Tears of the Midnight Soul

Seema Pillay

BookLeaf
Publishing

India | USA | UK

ACKNOWLEDGEMENT

This collection of poems would not have been possible without the support and inspiration of the many people who have touched my life.

First and foremost, I want to thank the countless souls I've encountered along this journey - those who shared their stories, their struggles, and their silent tears. Your experiences, both spoken and unspoken, have shaped the words on these pages.

To my family and close friends, your unwavering support has been a beacon of light in my journey.

I would also like to extend my gratitude to the poets and writers who came before me, whose works have been a source of inspiration and solace. Your words have guided me through many a sleepless night, reminding me that there is beauty even in the most sorrowful moments.

Lastly, to the readers of "Tears of the Midnight Soul," thank you for opening your hearts to these poems. I hope that within these pages, you find a reflection of your own experiences and a reminder that, even in the midst of sadness, we are never truly alone. Your journey through this book means more to me than words can express, and I am honored to share this moment with you.

With deepest gratitude,
Seema Pillay

PREFACE

In the quiet hours of the night, when the world is cloaked in darkness and the noise of the day has faded into a distant memory, we are often left alone with our thoughts. It is in these moments, when the stillness of midnight surrounds us, that our deepest emotions rise to the surface - unspoken fears, lingering regrets, and the soft ache of unfulfilled dreams. These are the hours when the soul weeps, not out of weakness, but out of an unrelenting need to be heard, to be understood, and to find meaning in the shadows.

"Tears of the Midnight Soul" is a collection born from these very moments. It is a journey into the heart of sorrow, where sadness is not something to be feared, but something to be embraced, explored, and ultimately, transformed. These poems are an intimate reflection of the human experience, capturing the raw and unfiltered emotions that we often hide from the world, and sometimes even from ourselves.

This book is for those who have known the weight of midnight, who have felt the tears that come without warning, and who understand the beauty that can be found in the stillness of the night. It is a testament to the strength found in vulnerability, and the quiet power of a soul that continues to search for light, even in its darkest moments.

As you turn these pages, I invite you to step into the quiet spaces of your own heart, to listen to the whispers of your midnight soul, and to find solace in the knowledge that you are not alone. For in these shared tears, there is a connection, a reminder that, even in our deepest sadness, we are all part of the same human story.

Depression

"The worst thing in life is not to end up alone,
but being with people who make you feel alone"

- Anonymous

She is scared, She feels shallow,
It feels the depth has vanished
Her inner self feels hollow,
Her emotions were banished

The footstep that follows,
Makes her crave for more
When she turns around to hold,
Disappear and leave her sore

She can't hear the raging storm
She can't smell the sweet rain
She can't hear the howling wind
She only feels the growing pain

The voices sound hoarse
Yes she had screamed and cried
Tried to find the source
To let the pain slide

She heard something, Oh its the silence
The silence so weird, so insane
Now approaching her
She is afraid she will never be back again...

Trapped

It hurts gently like the cold rain
I wipe them,
the tears rolling down
and yes, beyond recognition
lies my past
with mixed shades of pink and brown
where I stood at departure holding my faith
waiting for the moment
that never came
and will never come
because the verdict was announced
and there was a bedlam
and the fragrance of pain
is all over the air
so I get up and rise still in pain
because I am strong
to remind everyone
that strong doesn't mean no pain...

Distressed

"Sleep isn't just a sleep anymore, it's an escape"

- Anonymous

Teary eyes with Muffled cries
Strength lost and Hope dies
Cloudy skies bring gloomy nights
Meaningless love and painful fights

Lifeless body in its bereft soul
Confused mind with aimless goals
Choked heartbeats in a broken heart
Gasping for breath as truth unfolds

Raging fumes of Burnt wishes
Drift in air in direction unknown
No one to wipe the rolling tears
While wounded lies the soul alone

The Memory Lane

5

"I wish we could choose which memories to
remember and which to forget"

- Anonymous

Deep inside my heart I was waiting for this day
I brood as I try to cover the most painful crack,
as I lay
It's an illusion if you thought I would stay
You can't hurt me anymore, just like the
Moonglade

Ethereal Memories of this Ephemeral love
falling apart
Ripples of those memories emerge when I wear
that pink floral skirt
You never bothered to keep them fresh or repaint
for me

Some did not even last for one short second as
they vanished in the air
I become my own harbinger, my own Panacea,
only to make myself free
I carry myself away from the shore, as no more I
can bear

The distance keeps growing like an offing
Your fragrance gradually fading away from my
long knitted velvet gown
As I walk away, from you, your paths, your life,
I hear myself talking
I wow to never come back, I won't let myself
down

As the pleasant zephyr passes along
A crestfallen heart conflates with a carefree
sunshine to take charge of life again !

The Bereft Soul

"Monsters don't sleep under your bed, they
scream inside of your head"

- Anonymous

I am drowning in a cascade of thoughts
It drags me down towards a deceiving tranquility
Suddenly I feel encompassed by an unknown
fear
And hear a whisper in my ears, "hey, its me - the
depression..."

I can't make out the voice, it's so nebulous
I hate this moment when my fearless mind goes
hollow
I don't know where i am heading
But surely like hypnotized, i follow...

"Are you in pain?" Asked the voice
Something inside me said "Yes, i am. I don't
have a choice"
It poked again "Are you in pain?"
My fearless mind said "Why should I tell you,
what do I gain"

It nudged again "Are you broken"
I nodded my head, with words unspoken
Then it rained on me...
It crawled all over me making its way from my
toe to the head
Rupturing every memory that came its way and
left it bled

My secret sorrows are out, the world knows my
fears
I don't want to wake up now, i am in dearth of
tears
The mascara of my eyes is all over my face
Is there anyone who can help me see myself, no
- there is no trace...

The voice is gone far but left me with a feel
My wounds won't show anymore because my
heart is now sealed

Goodbye from her

"Love" - The reason I dislike that word is
because it means too much for me, far more than
you can understand."

- Anonymous

Her heart gone silent, a silence that hurts
She is happy but she is a little sad.
Trying to figure out all she really had

Got scars on her heart by touching few souls,
felt like she was dying
Only because she let herself scream without
even crying

Being madly in love and still not ready
But hanging in tight and holding it steady
She loved you in a way you have never been
loved and still not going to join you on the
bridge
She is drinking 3 kinds of poison and driving life
off the ridge.

Her heart goes through a slow death, shedding
each hope like leaves, until nothing remains

It will hold you up there till the last breath even
if that means that it pains.

Let her keep the last piece of her heart before
you tear it all apart.
Straining under the weight of all the lives she is
not living, sometimes she can hear her bones.
She now sees the difference between "living on
my own" and "being alone"

Been there now and then, now been here for
years.
The secret place she landed is known as the land
of tears
She smiles her sorrows away, still chained with
her past
Hurts her every time she says goodbye,
And you would never know which one is the
last.

Funeral of My Heart

"I am strong but I am tired"

- Anonymous

The day has come
To burn my heart down
Once which used to beat
Has turned to color of brown

Do come attend the funeral
And know what it feels
When it burns the memories
And leaves them to bleed
When it burns down the wishes
The fragrance it spreads
Making us realize
They were never read

When it burns the hopes
Stating nothing lasts for ever
While I made every second count
And still couldn't hold that hour

When it burnt the smiles
Filled with hopes

The ones i collected walking miles.
I bury them today with no regrets
I burnt my heart and cleared all debts

Did I need this ride
When I was never meant to be there
There is no place to hide
There are burns everywhere...

The more I long, the more I fade…

"The last time I felt alive – I was looking into your eyes.Breathing your air…. touching your skin…… Saying goodbye….The last time I felt alive…. I was dying."

- Ranata Suzuki

Following something that doesn't exist
Was it a wave that she couldn't resist
Happiness was a choice and she said never
Cut it open or stitch it back
you will always find it bleeding, because
sadness here lasts for ever

Moonlight gushing in through the vent
brightening a small part
But the brightness can't illuminate the darkness
that surrounds her heart
Living in a nightmare, more than often she
wakes up from sleep
With deep invisible wounds that are more
painful than anything that bleeds

She slips into empty spaces between words

She will disappear some day like flying birds
Thy cannot hold her in arms, but do hold her
memory in high regard
She will never be in thy life, but she will leave
her prints in the heart

Her irreparably broken heart will be broken
again
There is no real joy, anyway she wasn't here for
gain
She wants to turn around and tell the world she's
there
But she is moaning in sorrow not knowing
whether she will land safely or be scattered
everywhere...

The Waiting

15

This life is a dream,
a dream within dreams
Solitude is a painful reality that screams
Everything else is dreamDreams within dreams
With dreams without dreams
I serve a punishment without any endIn a
fathomless dark chasm
For a crime I didn't commit.
I follow the path without direction
Wherever it may leadScratching memories to
bleed

Gushing rivers of tears without an end
Every second pulls me closeto the never-lasting
hope of love and pretendThrough the Sparks of
twilight I Rose.

It hurts to read the words carved in my heart
I look around, but the darkness inside my eyes
so bright,
Darkens the brightest rays of light.
I still look back, in despair,
All in vain now because it's dark everywhere.

Fear Her...

I have seen her sadness last for ever
you would find when you look in her eyes
No one would ever know the meltdowns she had
she has cried the worst of the cries

the silent one
the one when no ones awake
the one that hurts the throat
the one that has the largest scream
the one that wont let her dream
the one that has no tears
the one that numbs all fears
the one where you hold your breath
the one thats worse than death

she has been through the unthinkable
so fear her when she looks at the fire and smiles
she arrived here after walking a million miles
she is the storm...

Living the Night

"People cry not because they are weak, but
because they have stayed strong for too long"

- Anonymous

Yes, I am living the night
For the world outside
But there is a storm raging
In my world inside

I am trapped in time
There is lot to settle
Does anyone care here
For my falling petals?

The color on me
Is the color of blood
If you let me open
I might even flood

I cant stay straight
I cant stand tall
I am ripped everywhere
I was meant to fall

Stained Rose

"Have you ever watched a rose as it fades away;
the color becomes deeper as the petals dry"

- Anonymous

Wow, they are fully bloomed,
Are they gonna die soon?
Of course!
Not everyone gets to be as lucky as Moon!
Wait, did they want to live longer?
Or did they want to live shorter?
Did they get what they wanted from life?
If not, hope they believe in afterlife!
Do they have any thorny regrets?
Do they have any fragrant confessions?
Did they want someone to pluck them?
Or did they want to be left alone?
Do you ever feel like one of them?
Or do you feel at home?
Oh, I see some black spots on the petals
May be its the sad part of their heart, do you see
those?
May be there are secrets hidden, who knows!

My Crushed Soul

19

I sat with my solitude and asked her,
Why is today more depressing than yesterday?

My sunless life daunting my present,
I am so much more in pain and dismay..
Terrified by what has come to my thoughts,
Horrified by what will come to me as a whole,
Nullified by what I stand as, in this world,
Petrified I look at the mirror and calm my bereft
soul...

Heartbroken and left in clouds of sorrow,
Greater than my faith, hides my fear in the dark,
Chilling my bones, Dampening my thoughts,
What is left, is no more going to ignite a spark.

Handle with Care

"There are kinds of pain that you can't speak out loud."

\- Jodi Picoult

If I said I am broken, will you handle me with care?
If I said it pains, will you help me bear?
If I said I am wounded, will you ask me where?
If I said I am sad, will you be around to share?
If I said there is a storm, will you help it calm?
If I said it's cold, will you make me warm?
If I said I needed support, will you be the wall?
If I said I was shaking, will you prevent my fall?
If I said I was scattered, will you pick me up?
If I said I was shattered, will you light me up?
If I said it's dark, will you be the light?
If I said I am scared, will you hold me tight?
If I said I might lose, will you help me fight?
If I said I am alone, will you be my knight...

Peacefully Blended

"Past is for reference, not for residence"

- Anonymous

As I dance here with you,
I let my heart go
As white clouds scudding across the blue skies
You emerge like a rainbow that peacefully
blended
The petrichor is driving me happy
I am here to embrace this life again
Your aurora is mesmerizing
I am truly in love with you, no pain
I have never pretended
I don't want to live in solitude anymore
There are colors of rainbow in the air
Fear doesn't tremble me anymore
I am bombinating like a bumble bee
The feeling is ineffable
The epoch with fears has ended
I fly above the clouds
Away from the past
I want to hold the moon
I am glad I m here at last
I want to look up high, I want to make it all right

I don't want to hold myself back
I have the power to change my world
Look up, the sky is not really black
Its the sun who goes down to brighten the stars
pearled
Look up high, it shines like sun in the night sky
Its not the sun, its the moon
See those stars who are twinkling to make
someone smile
Even the brume is going to go away soon
I am back to live life in the deep
I have found I got miles to go before I sleep...

The Forgotten One

"I feel my heart ache, but I've forgotten what
that feeling means"

- Chuck Palahniuk

Tears roll down like flowers from her eyes
She must have been through a lot
What looks like bunch of flowers to you
That might be all she got...

She holds the burden in her strong shoulders
Yes bravely, she has fought
The depth of her wound is beyond any
measurement
She is tied to her pain in the hardest of knots

Her heart bleeds and spreads the love
But the fresh cut wounds, beginning to clot
She stands tall to remind them of her
About her life - Half misused, half forgot...

Only if I could

"Only if I could go back in time to the place I met you...and walk away"

- Anonymous

Only if I could change the world that surrounds me
Only if I could see things the way you see
Only if I had the strength to overcome you
Only if I could bear the pain that always grew
Only if I could show you the mask I have been wearing
Only I could unload the weight I have been bearing
Only if I could make that one moment go away
Only if I could take back the words I shouldn't say
Only if I could bring back the days that made you smile
Only if I could make you once again walk that mile
Only if I could stop the clock from ticking
Only if I could hold this wound from sticking
Only if I could withstand the storm within

Only if I could forget with no regrets and once again begin...

25

Destroyed

"How happy is the Blameless vestal's lot! The
world forgetting, by the world forgot. Eternal
sunshine of the Spotless mind! Each prayer
accepted, and each wish resigned: "

—

Eloisa to Abelard, Alexander Pope

Should i forget you or remember you, I m not
sure
The pain is so brutal, it's not worth the cure..
If you can interpret it right, you have my consent
If you don't, I could be a penance, you will
repent

You be drunk if you take my sip
And I will happily be the reason to sink your
ship
Yes, I am here, with you and still being without
you
Displeased with myself, for something I already
knew

I can stay happy and still connect with all the
pain

I can live all the pain and still be closest to the
happiness rain
You may know me as dew drop…but
If you believe in me I will be the joy pop

Look at that dew drop, I am the storm in there
I am the undissolved venom of this universe,
beware

Your silence is the proof I am your guilt at the
peak
I am the obsession in you, that words can't speak
Why look at the start, that I am the result all
above!
What led me here? Regardless, now I am
destroyed in your love..

Feeling you Around

"The reason it hurts so much to separate is
because our souls are connected."

- Nicholas Spark

I can still feel your sillage in the air,
I still long for the times we spent in the woods
You were a magical trouvaille in my life,
how i wish i could steal you for good

Your sparkling eyes, your enticing smile is all i
wanted in those times.
When I pass by you every day now, it hurts to
know you will never be mine

I love you more than words can say, I love you
more than my songs can play
I love you more each passing day, all I wished
was that you could stay

Oh sunshine of my Life, the sea of my love, the
line of my fate, the beat of my heart
When you dance on my chest, the thoughts that
surge, melt me away and take the form of art

Memories of your Hug

"Sometimes a hug is an answer even is you dont
know the question"

- Anonymous

There is a silence around
But i am craving to hear that voice
The one that brought peace to me
The one that hasn't left me with a choice

The truth wants to burst out in open
But the fear holds its ground
My faith shakes from top to bottom
In a land of pretenders where truth is hard to be
found

Here comes my fear, Facing my faith on its face
I hold myself up high
I am hoping to win this race

A wish that i could have asked for
Has been granted without an ask
But all those memories i have gathered
Now will have to go behind the mask...

From "Being Your's to Been Your's"

"There is a silence around
But i am craving to hear that voice
The one that brought peace to me
The one that hasn't left me with a choice"

- Seema Pillay

Memories of your hug falling apart
Dark are those Meadows that once used to shine
But the stubborn mind refuses to accept
What had gone was never mine..
When the truth bursted in open
Those days were chilling cold
But we held on to the fear inside
Because those short hours were worth to hold
Never asked for that wish but it was granted
without an ask
In a land of pretenders i found joy in life
It came in like a thunder storm
And Left me with a lightening strike..
I was running alone
Running alone in the maze
Didn't realize I was running alone
And I thought I was going to win this race…